SHELMALIER

Medbh McGuckian
SHELMALIER

WAKE FOREST UNIVERSITY PRESS

Wake Forest University Press

This book is for sale only in North America.

Poems © Medbh McGuckian

First U.S. Edition published 1998.

Wake Forest University Press

Post Office Box 7333

Winston-Salem, NC 27109

ISBN 0-916390-86-1 (paperback)

ISBN 0-916390-87-X (clothbound)

LC Card Number 98-61113

Page layout by Peter Fallon

Contents

Author's Note *page* 13

PART ONE
Script for an Unchanging Voice 16
Dream in a Train 17
Pass Christian 18
Using the Cushion 19
The Sofa in the Window with the Trees Outside 20
Cancelleresca Bastarda 22
The Feastday of Peace 23
The Rose-Trellis 24
Sentinelle Perdue 26
The Sound Healer 28
The Word-Thrower 29
Cleaning Out the Workhouse 30
Circle with Full Stop 31
The Potter 32
From the Weather-Woman 33
The Feminine Christs 34

PART TWO
The Spirit Dolls 38
Man-of-War Bird 39
Pulsus Paradoxus 40
Rathlin Road 41
Their Word for Harvest Suffering 42
The Summer of a Dormouse 43
The Would-be Winter 44
The Field of Nonduality 45
Green Crucifix 46
Good Friday, 1995 47
Shoulder-Length, Caged-Parrot Earrings 48
The Third Chessplayer 50
Standing Army 52
The Building of the 'Hebe' 53

Mass Read by Night in the Open Air 54
A Blessing of Weapons 56
Cornet Love 57
Altar Girl 58
Arbalests and Mangonels 59

PART THREE
The Tree Cloud 62
Fox's Skin 63
Month Without an 'R' 64
Self-Portrait in the Act of Painting a Self-Portrait 65
Man Dressed as a Skeleton 66
Man with Pool Furniture 67
Man with Crossed Arms 68
War Masquerading as Love 69
Captain Heaven 70
Home Daughter 72
A Light Form of War 73
Habeas Corpus 74
Shelmalier 75
Tectiform 76
Foliage Ceiling Rose 77
Killing the Muse 78
Stone with Potent Figure 80

PART FOUR
The She-Eagles 84
La Bien Cercada; The Well-Walled 86
The Shadow Prize 87
Impressionist House 88
Blue Doctrine 90
White Magpie 92
The Brownstone Bride 93
Plague Song 94
The Shadow Lord 95

The Blood Changer 96
Praying Male Figurine 97
More than a Letter 98
The Sickness of the Cloth 99
The Jasmine-Picker 100
Columbarium 102

PART FIVE
Shannon's Recovery 104
The Latissimus Station 105
What the Month Brings 106
The Tamarind Tree 107
Creggan Churchyard 108
The Society of the Bomb 109
The Temple of Janus 110
Lake in Middle Shadow 112
Film-Still 114
Stone Orchard 115
The Birthday of Monday 116
Mantilla 119
Sky Portrait 120

for Patsy

Physical force may prevail for a time . . . but there is music in the sound of moral force which will be heard like the sound of the cuckoo. The bird lays its eggs, and leaves them for a time; but it will come again and hatch them in due course, and the song will return with the season.

— James (Jemmy) Hope
1746-1846
United Irishman

Author's Note

I owe the idea of this book to Jane Leonard, of the Ulster Museum, who suggested I should read up on the 1798 Rebellion with a view to writing a poem about it. I also owe a huge further debt to the new wave of researchers who have given us this centenary's version of what happened then. I found that what I had written in the form of epitaph and commemoration or address for the present-day disturbances in the North fitted like an egg into its shell that previous whirlwind moment when, unbelievably, hope and history did in fact rhyme. So the Victorian 'Shelmalier' with its beautiful coalescence of Irish and English, its sense of a lost and all but forgotten tribe, its being both a placename for a barony in Wexford and a battalion of seabird hunters, seemed an evocative title. The theme is less the experienced despair of a noble struggle brutally quenched than the dawn of my own enlightenment after a medieval ignorance, my being suddenly able to welcome into consciousness figures of an integrity I had never learned to be proud of.

Part One

SCRIPT FOR AN UNCHANGING VOICE

Script for an Unchanging Voice

Here is a stone with a stone's mouth inside,
a shell in which a lighter shell has died,

one with a honey bullet in its heart,
one that has lain full-length from the start.

The leaves are tongues whose years of blood are locked
in the wrong house, time feels unclocked

or has been dead too long by now to cast
its freshly slaughtered shadow from the past . . .

Dream in a Train

The world shovels snow
into a pond without an echo.
This image of water made visible
is a cry as warm as life.

The house is a perfect body
surpassing, unwriting me,
as the density of black repairs
light, even grows it.

Some part of my pine-wooded
mind sleeping or dead
was a tightened-up light
I was sheltering for years

which destroy something other
than flowers, eluding
by means of their own surface
the unchanging sea

around a swimmer
whose sigh is a fold
imposed upon the waves,
suggestive of an awakening.

Pass Christian

(where Newry is twinned with Clare)

I wish that sea-water would abstain from me now,
line after line of blue laws in civilian clothes.
Just flying, respectably dark, singing themselves to death,

they cut through the indigo roofline of my back
to the intestines, singling out the one thread
of my life where dry fronds rasp against each other.

Like a lip or spade, a scooping tongue or scooped ladle,
with nothing of the dryad or faun about him,
a twilight uncleaned from the day before
earned the eventual coolness of my love,
just short of harshness.

The insect-loud, four-faced war clocks
repeated the pips and cover name
of the fruit trains carrying strawberries north,
their extra-large windows powerfully possessing
the writing arm of space,
though here the fields did not stretch away.

Using the Cushion

The close-flowered orchid is more curious
than the few-flowered sedge: as though
the leaf edges formed a series
of rock steps into a saline cave,
where the air is not still, and a melanic
sky anastomoses, throwing out
lake-like arms to left and right:

or half-lake, half-river,
discharges veils of rain-widened
cutwater, over worn-down
knobs of slate, into newly freed valleys.

The Sofa in the Window with the Trees Outside

for Michael McLaverty

This weather — drinking champagne
on yellow satin, with gold forget-me-nots —
is unknown to me.
This green going out of the leaf
and summer brewing;
the frozen hedge lipped and flared
so every inch is thick
with a different flower,
not a flower escapes.

I had divided the waxen page in two,
like high pews from open benches,
believing what I still more believed,
to keep winter and spring distinct as hills.
But storm and blue sat under the one light,
or the feeling there is about a sky
when all lights but one go out.
And door and window fell upon each other
as if they were living, not speechless
with dust, more beautiful than any earth.

The dead among the spices of words
brush their eyes over me, as if
all my limbs were separate.
They are pearls that have got
into my clothes, they stir about
briskly with a form of tenderness
like a bird on its nest. I may
glide into them before they become set.

Their longing for conversation
upsets all the letters in my head;
now and then they turn off the lights
and look at the world: how white
fields can be on the first Sunday in Lent,
the way trees grow, in groups, how they
are bodily sunk to the lips
in the age of the garden.

I can see their rooms when the huddled moon
gets her week straight, dream after dream
like passing islands ringing
from the chaste night, their rhythm
destroys my rhythm
like a shelter around music,
or mornings in other people's houses.

They tell me something very warm,
something about a friend's life,
that fertile hour — that he had not,
then, been nothing; but they do not die,
as I do, with my air of rings widening,
or Satan joining my sentences
like two beginning lovers, with his hoof.

Cancelleresca Bastarda

Sleep made a market of my voice
like a night march through Connacht
or the sea's slack tides initiating.

I looked towards my father's voice
but saw only the first fruit-coloured
leaves, grooves on their inner and outer edges.

Half of him is lost on me
and on the trunk with its initials standing
creedless as a tesseract, on end.

The Feastday of Peace

Deep in time's turnings
and the overcrowded soil,
too familiar to be seen,
the long, long dead
steer with their warmed breath
my unislanded dreams.

View-thirsting at the wound-open
window, their weighted bending
down from a beclouded
day in the real past
runs a kind of springtime
through the air we will breathe.

Their lace-curtain Irish
anchoring the moon-lines
along the twisted sea-coast
chafes like a boat
in a sky-voyage the English
meaning so unlike language.

As summer's funeral
in the deceitful wane of the war
is like a paper bride
in an unwomanly room
touching her mildly widowed
newlywed body —

so these puritan fields
that could not give the answer
when the whole key of childhood
spoke like an eye —
were death fore-experienced
though the leaves were all there.

The Rose-Trellis

for Leon McAuley

If they destroyed all the words like electric light,
put them in a grave beneath branches,
could trees be expected to heal
without inherited things?
Would we be freed again like a view
seeing deep into seasoned gardens?

Without looking at me the trees
speak into this anxiously protected room,
their moving lips almost seeing
how they have lost their way,
how their lacelight is really
made of clouds.

Like a group of houses pearl-grey
in the grey, watered-blue in the blue,
they look words on to the lighted page,
though a summer night with stars is brighter.

They reach into the turning-over
bowl of the room, as if it were
extremely heavy,
into the drawer of the night-table,
into the dropped leaf of the secretary desk,
into the slanted pocket of my coat.

No place in the room is safe enough
to close itself back
over those still unused voices,
that slide from music
to soon-to-be-living words,
and bring back a kind of weak spring,

as if it had always stayed in the street.
It is so completely back inside it.

They cover the white sheet,
making addresses into dates,
they comb around and cling to my fingers,
and take up the line, then
put me back where they found me
like a piece of cloth.

Everything that more or less fits
is leaving the house,
slipping its third life on
as if it were inalterable,
like elastic girls whom birth has shattered,
each in a different way,
closing slowly in the warm housewinds
that forced them open and have fallen into them:
till the dense sound that wraps up
the meaning of an act of love
and cannot be cut, remains,
and stands up straight.

Sentinelle Perdue

Spring approaches, as it were, from afar,
a small deliverance, as if there had been nothing
between last autumn and this.

It ought to have been roused already,
the very, very tenderest green I know —
I call it snow.

I have not seen November, but I look
at little else: a face so sly and false,
it makes the sky-earth-sea come floating down.

To keep a sky clear, first these
have to be killed, then those,
then the last ones. Sandy grave mounds

in this colourful soil, before, in,
and after the rain, remain far below
the intensity of nature's greys.

Their Sunday-clean, untransparent ochres
show up how much light there is
even in this dusk. On the same day,

at the same moment, I too was walking alone,
feeling I was now on a road, though
the dreaminess goes out of it,

like a tide leaving the sea unchanged.
I was looking for blue all the time,
the least part-cloud or shade of it,

blue in the ripe corn or against a withered
beech hedge, blue enough to react to all
other colours, which have no more names

than threads have numbers. A shower of words
scourged the trees to a glorious warm black,
moss-roofed the cool garden, let a soft grey

speak in the tones of the same family,
so the highest light in that dolorosa brown
was her white throat next to the snowdrops.

The Sound Healer

1

The over-ripeness of your blistered doors
is a step I am frozen from taking;
my April sea-less eye stretches up
only to your windows. Your horizon
is a flat picture bent around a mug or plate,
your cloud structure is queueing up
for its second life in your heads.

Between meaning and meaning, matching words —
like husks protecting their insides from harm
or a halo of everlasting bluebirds swooping
inwards — carry the O no longer sheltered
under the arm of a T or in the fork of an F,
to the cross-marked roselight, the unshadowed green
that buried the most beautiful eyes in lime.

2

All is moving inwards and redder-appearing
than the innermost third of my May apple
filled from clear to black with old blood.

One thought-form away is the way for her
to leave. The benign neglect of her ovarian
voice is paler than the wood

of eighteen-year-old breasts, at hand-
warming height, their silver overspills
celestial in the tincture of time.

The Word-Thrower

These two fears unite us —
the deaths for which he is wrongly blamed,
the three people I know myself to have been.

The people he loves in the past are himself,
not a real person, not a ghost, my someone,
no one I had ever loved was real.

I heard my voice talking to the dream-voice
from the pillow; I let the days overlap and swim
out to sea, as though bitten by the past.

The less dark air and the shadows pair:
the light calms the air around the colours
that darken sweetly, little by little.

Cleaning Out the Workhouse

The rose unfolding at the corner of your mouth,
bare-rooted on paper, cries out to be kissed.

My heart in your mouth is a tan-coloured telephone
that hears your near-dying voice everywhere.

The curtains stream in the breeze, revel in sameness,
a human rookery outgiving the volume of life.

Your eighteenth-century fingers spice the soil
with blood and bone:

the leaves of my skirt separate and learn
the dead X in your name.

Circle with Full Stop

Birds are the only creatures who can feel
two things at once. I see and hear nothing
but the cheesemonger and chandler,
I've lain in the shallow dents where
sleep breaks all day with a pistol
by me, when I could have been swimming
under fire across the Danube.

But to bring out the taste of the month
I've had my dive into your head
where it was summer till three-thirty
and always afternoon.
In the dance of the months I was August,
now I've gone back into winter clothes,
a March sea, the glacial white of the reading-room.

I am pinning together a chair-cover
from the flaring fragments of your shirt,
drawing my hands to and from my lips
like dusk adding truth to the chain
of pictures lining the house.
When sleep flings its inkstand, everything
is a few degrees clearer.

The Potter

To my word spouse
I was not Eve nor Helen,
not Mary nor Sophia,
but the fool of the house.

He followed my breath
and left it in the face
of one who was pronounced dead
by the history of faith.

I sit in the lotus
of courtly love,
in the locked dialogue
of errors outlived

and deny that he is
all spices commingled,
with my entire body sown,
deny that he is light.

From the Weather-Woman

Not even a dead letter
a pseudohope from your pseudohome.

You are dissolved in me
like the death of the century.

I need your summer movements
as the spirit needs the world,

my non-world the inner
gospel of your letters.

From the unhardened nature
of the memories, your prison

look, that mood, that number,
leads a road where nothing

can unhappen, to the meeting
of two opennesses: the one

I write before the visit,
the one you will write after it.

The Feminine Christs

Christmas Day, 1996

Their pulses are differently timed, mule-
powered, safely poured in two directions
into time, into the collected object.

All their fingers are together, they are
tight-lipped, unwakeable mothers
embraced to the hilt and reconceived.

Whom persons, unwed, now identified
in marble, looking small enough
to take in one's western arms.

Wounded tables decorated with autumn
leaves, planked streets, desolately
curved roads, unhappy anythings.

Every star is an upper self
that half-hangs down out of the heated
audible blue behind them.

Their dreams churn in the midyears
from century to century, their bought
books are a sharp green hedge.

It would be better to turn round
and say 'The Spring', or any other
whole-hearted not sincerely.

If ever you wanted to buy a museum,
to see whether a gentle snowstorm
always filled with moving

could seem natural, turn to a new altar,
a stronger faith and a weaker life,
reach to the last drop your virtue.

Part Two

THE SPIRIT DOLLS

The Spirit Dolls

They subtract us as matter from their lives —
spice-merchants, tanners, coopers, weavers,
wine-merchants, innkeepers, florists, casual mercenaries.
They made themselves up as they went along,
their cross-streets linked in city wards,
the Parish of Hospital, in the Diocese of Emily.

Authentic children of the Covenant, my anti-family,
my anti-home, my counter-home, residence
is being conferred on them, a homely dress
that they have donned, as insiders' outsiders,
as a new us and an old them, in the scoured pot
of our acid, indigestible, please-and-thank-you army.

And now, from their eerie inland sea, from water
house or drowning cell, a species of anti-workers,
anti-bodies, professional loiterers, ne'er-do-wells,
emerge corrected, dusted by clandestine truce,
like the reputed male, 'Semper Augustus', red flames on white,
to avoid turning out as a nation, turning into a state.

Man-of-War Bird

What do you sing behind the music
on the street side of the street
that never slept?
Your much-concealed silhouette
turns the room's deliberate dark
into a sweet-briar island,
where conflicting window-light
deadens the windows, filling them up
until they breathe together.

It could be this year's kisses
or any kind of love locked
in the bars on the wings of the chaffinch,
or the arms of the earliest woman.
Your face that dressed itself
free of everything except beauty
and was open like a shelf
from the beginning
changes all my pictures of the air:

so a Freedom Box on a soldier quilt
seems a hat nesting on a black bed,
and a slow broom against my white
shoes in a summer kitchen,
recalls a Red Throated Diver
crowned in his winter plumage.

Pulsus Paradoxus

At first something like an image was there:
he had for me a pre-love which leaves
everything as it is. We do not see everything
as something, everything that is brown,
we take for granted the incorruptible
colouredness of the colour. But a light
shines on them from behind, they do not
themselves glow. As a word has only
an aroma of meaning, as the really faithful
memory is the part of a wound
that goes quiet.

Keeping magic out has itself the character
of magic — a picture held us captive
and we could not get outside it
for it lay in our language in the uniform
of a force that no longer existed.
Peace was the target he was aiming at,
the point at which doubt becomes senseless,
the last thing that will find a home.

Rathlin Road

There was a low-spreading blazing blue
on the surface water that re-fought the battles:
a never-ending red rinsed in green,
little-understood, a colour we scarcely knew.

We were a tiny island of women
being sung to sleep on an island of talk.
Years without speech or cries of absence of mind
had lessened our minds, our calls close to song.

Always rain and only rain freed me,
I would lie like new water after it,
in an after-image where dust had not collected,
hoping the wind would pick me out of the earth.

Bleached gold the clouds bent back
and purpled on and off, never again
to seem old. The east-west path
so magically cooled shed the foursquare day.

Like a telephone too filled with voice,
a living argument beneath an agreed window,
the heavy seasons co-operated with the map,
and near-Parisian weather salted our Christmas eyes.

Their Word for Harvest Suffering

I prayed to my imperfect idol freedom
till roads and rivers moved, limousine lanes
tilted into roadlessness. To my night-thirst
even the weather was a secret glaze on water,
the trouble-free future at the red street corner
split plum-soft, as if it were an organ of my body.

The over-garrisoned city still looked like
a capital. Triple kissed by the calm
on land which is found at sea — who
were we, standing five deep, shoulder
to inner shoulder, easing ourselves like stars?

The Summer of a Dormouse

The roses tall as girls
at their fullest stature
among my books and sabres
were my less-loved lesser sister.

The unburnt stars
sleepwalked in my half-grave
windows; bowls spouted
ribbon-handles in the waters' growth.

And the child that is always missing
buried his rounded mouth
in my breath-coloured rim
like a partial cremation,

till his long unborn voice
emptied the fill of the shaft
into the rose-late skirt-coat
of the lake's divided flag.

The Would-be Winter

The storm colours and the outer purple
of your stronger eyes laid my essence down
as bone. Peace waves and fresh war winds
indivisibly fought about clouds.

The war-drunk war-weather
was the messenger that excites
the almond ovary, till the plant beckons
with young flowery twigs

like black petticoats vibrating
pure oxygen — pure blood — a bouquet
of dumb pathways letting a word
flow written into the hearing cup.

The Field of Nonduality

Like a map your lips promised,
when melancholy creased you,
apron and rash and savage
uplift of stones.

You pressed the path into place
and improved it, every step
a brake, your eye
a stride away from your foot
on the breast or intake route.

By plucking threads
from chair covers sprinkled with bees,
seeing through dry mist
in native trees
lanterns of fishing-smacks
swaying on thin masts,

you uncurtained a certain mountain
from a certain other,
walked off the edge of the torn map
on to another.

Green Crucifix

for Seamus Deane

A month and a half of rain:
I have been counting heavily.

Now the incense beats at my door,
he is there by the hour, my joyful
fighter.

There is no need to shape
his breath, I can feel his breath's
smoothness, its sparkle, its flavour.

The two deep creases of our wedding-rings
change in touch; I place the same
red on his lips

unwilling to see the remembered
blue of the river in his seated dark
whose black cuts across my arm.

My hands in balletic positions
glove his ungloved hands, the skin
resistance of his missing backbone

in the abandoned sheets. And like
two choiceless Christs,
our side-swept feet

shaded by straight masts,
that the Resurrection's steadiness
would never get clean.

Good Friday, 1995

The builders seem to have clapped
one town on top of another:
a marble summer mirrors
the imperial blue.

Mass-bound women
leave their own doorsteps after dark
and feel the childlike dew
of the illuminated garden.

They make netted purses
seasoned by warfare,
shoulder knots from circlets
of black marigolds,

pistol-whipped
thread-paintings
to lay soft-eyed
by his cold side.

Shoulder-Length, Caged-Parrot Earrings

Female eyes — male hand — head full of closed sky —
your throat is still open, though your blood is being dried;
the clock you started up in me, leaves the plainest roses
barely aged.
        You play a secret set of muscles
to bring up a rifle to your cheek, your nights
billow no more than truces, swimming towards daylight.

How lightly then your rich body weighed — tonight
it weighs even less — lowflying as meadow-coloured lead
overflying the white ruin of waves, their feeble climaxes
sucking spring from the ground, a nude beach whose skin
rings out like an Angelus in foliage.
        Instead of my Communion watch,
I read the hour in the stubble of your beard.

And *now* begin to live, like a too faithful people, whose last
conquered hamlet has ceased signalling.
        Bastille Day
weather covers me like waltzing one-horse towns,
caught in ice, or seeds in mad acceleration, Europe-bound.

Your arms are a living robe of earth you halve
with me so death is a quarantine — only half a death.

You hold me like an unlit cigarette, while you burn
match after match, offer yourself in vain.
        You run
star-splashed over the rust which would have gushed
through your hands, six-months' obscure sap-thrust
halts the coastline of your so-called 'sea-girt isle',
so-habitable province, serving up its ultimate smile.

The small green plant in the wound on your wrist
became the lens through which I saw how air could pierce
the ground: how black clouds fattening were slave-joys
you rejected.
      Flight-cramped child, hollowed into airworthy place,
your lingering future is less meditated-necessary
than to sail this eve-of-battle, national holiday, sky.

The Third Chessplayer

for Barrie Cooke

He pulled me into the fierce summer south
of his voice. He plunged me into the present people
against the past, a dozen different weathers,
crisp days, full days, keen mornings.

With his other head he sheared away
the rope-marks on his back, leaving it markless,
swirled the ice in the teeth of snow,
controlled how the busy heat of autumn's care

fled the ground. The regret of having
to remember shabby war years flung me
decades back before the sidewalk tables
replaced the winter barricades.

I drove north his morning and his evening,
in late p.m. like the first swallow
I agreed to April. Once I lay across
his wrist in the apron of shade,

hearing the bone-lipping sound of an enlarged
heart massage the tone of parting.
His inbreathed air was my drug of choice
and in every inch of his tender throat

I was running into sleep or its pretence.
In one clean break, a handmade knife-cut,
we became violently two again.
Like a single cloud in its ring, with just

a few gestations left, he drew the flower's
flame and odour into the almost-clear-sky
coloured bowl, a brother to the smooth brown,
rich green page of the mutual earth.

Standing Army

The place is considered gentle, unprovincial,
though small boats cannot live in it,
a post town where virtue means
anti-government like any natural wood.

I love to read the breast water
of his body under meadow,
the jewel of his identity
in the river's summer depth.

With his head towards the west,
at the cardinal points of the day,
the unlettered headstone rings
when touched by any other stone.

A bugle re-echoes in four caves,
each on a different key, and more
unmelancholy there, six notes, three low,
three loud and rapid, the hornblende Irish cry.

The Building of the 'Hebe'

You blanket the door with a faithless shuddering,
having stripped off the entire bark of a tree
while all the dew was on.

We walk dry under its coverlet
to the opposite hills with their different iron colours.

Higher and higher the tearless grass
opens a window under my feet,
and quite across my mouth, leaving the smooth
meadow where my house stands all entry,
like a fungus, in a coarse snarl.

The shade trees before it
underlie the summer there
and make the yellow soil express
its unreaped summer's thought

that this harbourless coast, my harbour
for the season, is profaned by an alburnum boat
injuring eternity by the edges of its channel
as if the waves had planted it for coves and inlets;

it ruptures the sand foliage
where no sand was to be seen before,
with smeared lips on which no beard grows,
but the blood of winter flaming

so land-locked a vase, to flood the growing
moon, in the angle of a cloud,
whose ice-grain some had trusted for a cloud,
through rafters with the bark still on.

Mass Read by Night in the Open Air

Light actually passes through
the points of expensive locks.
The fertility of uncounted hours
perfectly broken into one another
crosses time as if it were a room.
And my yellow life
with its downy blacks
takes rainbow widths of grey sky
from the first inverted flames
of the dewy turn of his wrist
into the purple that bees love.

On my knees as generations before me,
fleeing a dead city,
I was the set-faced silence under
the breast-moulding sparkle and airy system
of the mile-high branches.
Face downward before the wind-angel,
he sang a dozen notes with his nude throat
into the piano, in the space of an hour,
that sharply played against that living time,
stopping it as it began to blunt.

Though one side of his body still
feared a blow to the nape of the neck
his back lengthened and widened and opened,
his right shoulder, that had been mistaken
for a pillow, moved apart in a bite,
not held narrow but allowed to spread.

He hovered like a guarded crown
that skimmed the band of turbid clouds
collected there in the trees.
And walking through their falling flames
that till then had been but of one colour,
we chose this Up, not where the ceiling is.

A Blessing of Weapons

He fires joy-shots out of view
of the audience — the same four songs
each night for over nine years.

Do I have the right to kill a blade
that rusts and consumes its scabbard
till it is wedded to dry land,
working at less than oyster-power,

every educated muscle so hulked,
he in his wider circles thinks
a dense patch of star, a moon
or two my inmost paradise?

If I belonged to the place
as I wanted to belong
to the small-scale war, the army town,
the three-act, one-day battle,

instead of the harrying treaty
of oblivion, using different muscles,
I would be reading, *ventre à terre*,
that number, my street address as a child,

why they kept our names on the signs
describing the massacre.

Cornet Love

So I close my unmilked kiss for you
inside the harp-embossed bullet mould —
so I dip my tarnished pen three times
in the silver sepia of your cooling swanshot —

should I carve out something less flawed
than the set of six lilac chairs
wrapped in the bull's hide of a charred
chasuble, half-a-year in sleep,

a crescent of counties cultivated to the top?
Having to live entirely in the eye
of Europe, coffined in a thin penal
shell, like sill-deep water parted from the sea,

we would tear into each other's smoothest turf,
one hand as an anchor, one on your flamespread
body, the two of us astride
the one horse shoed from south to north.

Then would all the muses drink
from the fragrance of the same cup
the undermost red of the double
and the single touch, where the decade

hinges into the visible century,
a fire lit with the kind of wood
that symbolizes how you think
to the point where it would not burn me.

Altar Girl

He is wearing that tumultuous tablecloth
among the unclothed women. His hands
are out of view, but the whole line
of his cranium is exposed from the temple,
fabled earmarks, a cavalier's skull
hammered from within like the stamped
gold of a crozier.
                         Her irisation
pays his interior court,
drenched in his perfume, in fields with him,
or on a wide sandy road where dawn
has caught them somewhat apart.

They no longer have the wall behind them,
his colour is wholly used up
by her flat brown extending the sky's
stinging rhythm.

The century turns its new keys
in a cross whose centre is not there:
with the sleeve of a man who has lost an arm
he opens that thousandth door.

Arbalests and Mangonels

From the Feast of the Assumption
to the octave of Saint Martin,
shock-troops unhorsed the spear-forest.

A chaplet of half-living flowers
hammered the mailed yew,
and a garland of periwinkle
after the new guise, three times over,
substituted its blood-price for law,

leaving not so much as a finger-bone
of the much-vaunted peace
when the sun-dried skeletal hand
fell pointing from its appointed place.

Part Three

THE TREE CLOUD

The Tree Cloud

Light shot like the jerk of a chain,
a hand distributing all that was warm in him:

boughs bent inward to their trunks,
firm snow under the wing
belonging to a grey angel.

Your lips stung
with the stained whiteness of loose-hung
windows in a room that sent its ray
in a conscious path across
the earlier night.

Fox's Skin

Now you have stopped the movement
of my outgoing breath with yours incoming,
I offer my breath into yours as a sacrifice.

The inside of a breather is a double well,
white-rimmed, druidic, one book's poverty
flowing into the world-knot of the other.

My garden of desire trees is older and more clothed
than your perfectly rounded field, a line
comes out of you into God's hands as a thread.

Month without an 'R'

Before the moon was an hour down
another death intruded,
like a handkerchief frozen stiff
beneath a pillow.

A stream of lives flowed
in the black cotton of mourning,
the current of the years ahead
rushed the sick winter
to its last word.

The convict band unsought in chains
played in the square;
the island stumbled into false quiet,
or something approaching evening.

The warships in the haven
spangled a giant frozen wave
of gunfire waiting for the rain
to change its mauve colour.

Grey warming into brown
slept badly and dreamt well:
a patio rose, frozen like a coat
to a common door.

Self-Portrait in the Act of Painting
   a Self-Portrait

Unreadable day, you must have sat
too often by the dying. Cracked window,
of no property, you must have heard
the busy tinkle of blood.
Never youthful light,
with the minimum of heat,
you collar whole walls
in the feel of trampled flower-ness,
you traverse the city from end to end
in the sky's safety,
to an outer position of a double
circle of positions,
where her Musehood has withdrawn
into a single drop.

The striped gown she lifts
without the painting looking
is the edgeless gunboat surface
on which we all exist.
Each dusting scrapes an internal winter
from her summer missal, like self-caressing,
long-folded clothes, of a sailor
home from sea.
And no answering of seige
but her ears closed and her lifetime's gaze,
the forced glint of a real pupil
through the inferior blue,
on her own reflection, undigested,
in the fruit with their dismembered trunks
of faces.

Man Dressed as a Skeleton

I look back to a valley just left:
the cropped gold end of a forest fire
springs a black rainbow in a church's ground.
Pastel blue water pounds
the well-washed island
to come out lacy on elaborate stones,
and seven lipsticks dry
the unwanted morning's lipped feeling
to a moon-responsive day whose
white-inside hinges keep blushing
where melted silver poured down
the throat of a subject race.

I sat counting your alphabet
on the loved-outside of my dress:
your head's opposite ways smelt of grass,
your eyes lavished no guiding shine,
your fingers avoiding my breast were turquoise
drops on a stem. The light of soft, expensive kid
came down too low to form a prettier noose
in the cluttered passage of birth and first words.

But your back going in made an almost-well
floor, no flowers had smell
like the deeper flowered whole red rose
completely in red flower
that basked like four roses in my throat,
still in my neck. Or gently lashed
like an old but open tree that began
down somewhere Greek and low.

Man with Pool Furniture

We look redemptively
like the utterly reasonable moon
through a window in eighty-six parts
at the screen-lovemaking
of his hammocky shroud.

A mock chapel,
where the beautiful duties of the body
coat his nipples with the oil tincture
from the cones of the retina,
so his lake suffers no silt.

The metal samples
in the salt reflections of his hair
wed two colours to a Bible blue,
Saint Barbara reading
with her back to a fire.

I carry like a Saint Christopher
in my incurable care
his ring made from a spoon,
the word you pouted gracefully
as before candles supersensually blown.

Man with Crossed Arms

A sun-filled pocket that becomes a burning space,
your shoulder's east lip, the gateways of your face,

like glasses and plates that talk among themselves,
a collapsed door, and a furlong of laden shelves.

Your mouth of fire blouses like the coldest, whitest skull,
more faithful than the pulled-closer road which hugs the hill,

you hold my natural hand to bend behind a skyless tree,
the blue of your wing hovers high and folds in me.

War Masquerading as Love

How often is he to be buried
with a flower at his lip
and a vase as his pillow?

Far be it from me above ground,
when a bird's head flaps,
to thread as many as three rings
on the finger of my wish,

that a child has crawled
on to the shroud,
and bent a sword-blade
around his neck,

so the spectre takes on
sweet forms, the male
grain or the female vine.

But something as trivial
as heating water flares
an open and urging fire
from my shoulder to my lip:

to be handled or serve as
quarry or pass as a field
stone through known gates
into his urn-field.

Captain Heaven

The erect flag lifts from its emptiness
like a masted boat, a pyramid balanced
on its apex, or a tie that has worked free
into a blowy sky.

I fasten one to my easel, it touches the canvas
at various points, draping it in an inoffensive
light-green churning, as if a whole month's
history of Ireland were fainting into leaf.

Now it is a rose lying on his arm, that settles
into a pool of ruby rust about the back
of his head; a rose-coloured membrane
that wanders coarsely on the rim of his coat;

a little pennon of gently purled and slender
feathers where his elbows break out,
that brushes his clothes from neck to ankle;
a banner of tossed blue, that *nolens volens*

brings a feeling of the air to the tilt
of his arms. His left hand is casual,
as though expecting fruit, and his unemployed
hand gathers up the countryside

on the nipple of the pistol, its halfness,
in his pocket. There must be a path
up from the sea through his legs firmly apart
in the dockscape, two sets of steps

opposite each other as they rest between acts.
The day has moved on some hours
but seems to find its horizon in moments
of yellow mauve with heather and gold,

with gorse on his forehead and Bedouin instep.
Immediate as a cloud, I lay my dark dress
like a living part of a letter posted wordless
thirty years later among weapons in an imitation tomb.

Home Daughter

Ever-refreshing golden upper sky,
twelve heads from a frieze are brushed on to you
just like a morning kiss, just whitening
with winter passage rain.

Graded sky devoted to justice,
seventeenth-century people from a red-figured vase
become your monthly furniture,
give their names to your clouds.

A cylinder of moving human beings
confiscated from a Sung bowl
cut off the King's English sky with a knife,
look at lands on a marriage tray.

A Light Form of War

Lean back, take a small step backwards,
form a T with your hands and practice
your surrender. Your stillness is your gift,
a silver chain that stains the trafficless
snow of my neck, its low touch
low-sexed and boyish. Your newly relaxed
muscles ripple towards bitterness, the first
oddly lit colour of the final spadeful.

From the mid-stripe in the road, a wall
of clear light makes a round shot
to defend you and a lining for your coffin.
In the waterlight I am rose-cut
by the spotless dryness of your soul —
and all of this can happen in this world.

Habeas Corpus

The page is torn between Sunday and Tuesday —
the heretofore, the up-to-date hereafter.
Glass-blue kisses turn the twilight to scatter
over my smoothed-down, freshly-minted skin,
the ringlet lines on your wrists new-faceted to sun,
your older shoulders quarrelling with my younger breast.

But you will be the watcher of my undereye darkness,
my garment without pockets, you will never escape
your shrine. Nightlong, your bare, blanched altar
will tell my quietened breasts white from white.
No blood velocity will rust-proof your heart
from the shallowest underbreathing of your chest.

Cloud growths lapping up on every outbreath
tunnel the counter-revolutionary morning:
a bruise-like feeling eases your bitter horse-girths.
Your neck sustains your head as if it needed
no sustaining, you draw to the blown sand of your body
my dream-track iced like every man's doorstep.

Shelmalier

Looked after only by the four womb-walls,
if anything curved in the ruined city his last hour
it was his human hands, bituminous, while all laws
were aimed at him, returning to the metre of a star:
like a century about to be over, a river trying
to film itself, detaching its voice from itself,
he qualified the air of his own dying,
his brain in folds like the semi-open rose of grief.
His eyes recorded calm and keen this exercise,
deep-seated, promising avenues, they keep their kingdom:
it is I who am only just left in flight, exiled
into an outline of time, I court his speech, not him.
This great estrangement has the destination of a rhyme.
The trees of his heart breathe regular, in my dream.

Tectiform

Oh my genetically youngest
child-fabric, unshepherded navel.

Concentration of a plant's potency
in your horizontal listening.

Green leaf weighted down
with a handful of earth:

there is no food on which your shadow
opening its swell pedal
does not fall,

my non-belief
in the virginal afterbirth
of your body.

Foliage Ceiling Rose

This shallow brook breaks death into two.
The divine perfume of the purest of the dead
buys this freedom.

My headless convict-doll
has the mouth of someone spoiled,
whose glance stumbled against,
not grazed, mine.

There is a distance in motion
between his face and mine,
sudden lapses from Italian into French
between madam mirror and her shadow,
her oath-helper, her hooded character,
and the judge who hovers lovingly
over the accused.

I want to be finished with this legend,
this bitter need to mock virility
by mocking language.

But there are no remedies, I hope,
against the atrocious flavour of the war,
except a low mass said
in a Spanish-held town
with the old words, nocturnal,
like women, the words which are mine.

Killing the Muse

My crucified girl,
my Zeus, Satan horns
skin-deep in your oldest cry.
I re-cut your name-to-be
among herbs and lavish gold.

No living woman
was more alive in her sleep, my
least alive of flowers.
Day alone takes your place,
unfinished nightpiece.

It was my first small anguished
crucifixion, the fresh blood drifting
from the last quarry into perfume
spoons, an afterlife
that thinks and knows.

I am shaken by the stormlight
closeness, the closer and closer
wrapping of marble
around your trance-bound body;

I crush my fists
in fringing pleasure
against your lowered eyelids,
their browns that were not shade.

Earth that forced
the fruit to enter
is disappearing
from the landscape.

In your smileless mouth,
a sign of two lips,
a parted male tongue bleeds.
A split-off bone is loosed
from your neck like a pearl necklace.

No one is looking at anyone
if we interlock our fingers,
not to pray,
or your whole body turns to body forth
its underworld of shell-bronze breastplates.

Stone with Potent Figure

My inward country slept
an oak south of the third furrow,
giving the wild bees
sugar from her fingers
in their shy approaches to communion
with her coaxing hands.

The wind blew in circles
through the isles of the trees
as it will under a mountain,
painting the pivot counties
grey in grey as independent
as dependent men.

Her head to the west,
her legs to the east,
her black-stained left arm bent;
the waist front of her skirt
a very clumsy seam along
the slightly constitutional fields.

Beneath her a frond of bracken,
the wings of six jackdaws
and two crows, twelve small wings
and four large, three
crab apples on the breast
over her light-loving heart.

There was a fall of semi-pure
earth, but the lid fitted
so tightly, not a speck of soil
had worked its way within,
only a little heather, moss,
a birch leaf at the root end.

Her bones were reduced to a pale
blue powder that the dried muscles
held like thongs; her grave
no more than a low
unworkable bank
of cultivated disbelieving.

That she herself was buried
weaponless in her coffin
in that summertime I know
from the flowering head of yarrow
laid with care by her right knee —
carpenter's or soldier's wort, a cure for possession.

Part Four
THE SHE-EAGLES

The She-Eagles

War-bred birds circle above
the leaf-roofed water
like half-tender wolves of the sea.

Their mouths are purses,
they strike the water singing,
with the underside of their heads,
as loud as their heads can hold,
so the whole night seems to feel them.

No fond cloud
draws death upon herself so badly,
with the help of the moon.

Their breasts torn open,
they graze the dark wall,
the narrow arm of the river's fullness,
where the tide makes itself felt
from mouth to mouth,
and the water can no longer be drunk.

A breeze with a developed voice in it
utters smoothly,
speaks to its unshaded,
snowy self.

They take the words up
as from lips,
pouring off at intervals
the outer rings of blood
in the manner of snow freezing blue
on a war Christmas.

But the English words refuse to breathe
and two spread hands
make the cell-learned Irish
a semi-jail at prayer.

There's a white silk gap
in the given language
where close-packed graves
and their slow-waved sleep
set in glimpsed bronze the sister words
so willed they become a food.

La Bien Cercada; the Well-Walled

Like birds that return to a tomb yearly,
shoals of slow soft rustling convent clouds
split their aching distances to form a sort of mouth
or little smouldering gold window in your chest.

Our two tongues, two churches, placed like a gift,
blossom like a building delighted into life
with the scarlet splashes of poppies through soil
we both have ploughed, through land fit for dances.

A certain martial rawness in the male gaze
of the Muse-sacred roses with no longing left
grafts you like a black limb onto my white body,
though I won't hold your head's temple grapes again.

You are drawing me, sword-bearing Saint Catherine,
with your non-dominant hand the twelve inches
to my mother's eyes, those sawn stars said to sing
and broaden from their seven pains at dawn.

The Shadow Prize

In scarlet eggs in a gold-brown train
of wool-backed, satin-banded snail shells,
the war had sealed us off. We lived over
every page those deeply carnal
moments indescribable as voices are.

Each tree had the profile of a man's face,
near enough to arouse and betray.
The fear I felt at the otherness
of his calm life inched me wide
like a door left open for him.

The equal-armed cross seemed to pour
towards me. I would wreathe him around
the smallest curve of my neck, tie him
with sea-marks to the tense recurve
of my mast, as winter towards moisture.

A chain of rings all magnetised,
and sung not as songs learned,
slipped his luxuriance into place
like a commandment in a gilt frame,
sunless and beautiless, on the far side of his name.

Impressionist House

1

Just because there is a blue sky in the background
these loves are not for everyone's understanding.

See them against the blue, in the blue even,
you will tell me that mountains are not like that,
a glooming over-admixture of restless black,
the voice of the wheat sun-steeped
in the furnace of harvest-time's height.

The first person who came along and felt the spring
so deeply was a nude man, realistic,
leaning against a door into a rich interior.
I exaggerate the fairness of his hair, his leisure
for love-making, the tinting French air,
the half-broken tones of his face, the languid postures
of his clumsy hands and arms like claws.

That difficult bottle-green majolica jug
represents the eternal nests of greenery
for lovers, built with eggs of violet glass,
where, luminously asleep, so the sky itself
colours him, the years count double for
my necessary, palatable, prisoner-of-war.

2

Father-brother, elder brother, feeling instead of me
the medal of the Virgin round your neck,
your sudden 'not-ready' smeared rain all over
the skin of my summer-dark window.

If the fields of my night are parched,
yours are too wing-to-wing for sleep: if your self-
addressed letters are the only light under
my door, I am your costly and fallible sleep-flower.

An Anglo-Saxon word for shade or enclosure
hidden like powder enough for ten evenings
through the ranks of the men of the streets —
cup with two handles on either side, two lips.

Blue Doctrine

The boundary of the light will not coincide
with the edge of the window.
With me by his side he is not compelled
to think about me,
nor would he care
whether my lips were more or less red.

I feel like breaking the enchantment
with a fierce shout, rendering needless
the deception of colour, or writing
each sentence in a different colour
so it resembles a little flag,
having for background a half-sun.

For those who sit in the darkened
doorways of their dwellings devoid
of doors, the trouble-adding sound
of bells can mean whatever you want
it to — mobilization, a warlike tempo,
passive defence.

Over my head a bat unfolds its wings
like hands that seem to seek
each other's warmth, or an eyelid
opened in the pulse of a glove,
as in the coat of arms
of my native city.

The air of the first night of summer,
not a moment too early, not a moment
too late, leaps into my paper bed
in the uniform of sleep
from the waist
down.

First a long stretch, then mistakes,
then jumping by tens, until his stomach
is tight against my thighs, ending
in a row of noughts,
as if he had been with a woman.

White Magpie

The black beams overhead,
they had been birch, pear and willow wood.
Remember well their blood-tunnel perfume
as it enters the refuge of your lips,
for a forest is a highly-perfumed dungeon,
hate-crested, gold-skinned,
a portable Tudor prison.

The prisoners, with washed faces,
were walking aft, one by one.
Will the slaver,
wearing the ring of her anchor,
be allowed to go to pieces where she lies,
moistening the blossomless sea-sand,
calmly waiting for the Angel Death?

Almost every head was uncovered
by a willingness to come out
and see a pageant pass;
a musk-duck swayed over
the off-horse Fleur-de-Lis
and stars, unknown before, kissed
his right cheek through the white cap.

My best river breathed an hour
after the dexterous stillness of the rope
and the smaller dark-pea thongs
down the wrists in front of the stomach
ceased beating the air.
Who will now buy the great ocean
avenue of his sodden necktie?

The Brownstone Bride

I was beginning the next but two chapter devoted to him,
his mellow-vespered masculine voice, the lighted
centre of my story. Not a death-night touching
my sleeve, but my active, operative germ of self
lacerated and untended, on the peopled-enough sea,
a life led in trees by the sore and sterile
unresting imagination, trapped in vigilance forever.

Then a weariness, deadly, deep and inconceivable
as a necklet of turf I wore with shame,
spent its paired evil around me, and from too far off
I read a little dustily the unloved lines of names
like an *éclopé* glimpsing the rush of men —
a winged glance, a final view
separated by one field from the sordid path.

My bed so made, and breathing some pacification,
it was the strangest state to have lived on and on for,
a mistime of fond confused signs, an acknowledged lover
by whom you most want to be understood,
holding a full-held polite door shut,
neither repairing nor preventing the painful dividedness
of my woman-closing, obligatorily mated arms.

I know at last these incomparable pages
by heart, and him only readable again
as the world swings clear of sorrow, and we talk now
of balm, its forever and ever, almost to a like tune,
for all the stones that that will replace.
Our time has been these lesser known, better months,
and more and more never apart, the reproduction of the note.

Plague Song

Torso of music on the crutch of Irish —
this is the netted green in you,
marching and counter-marching,
requiring two separate orchestras.

Already under sentence,
with autumn at your centre as well
as at your edges, the join between
the centuries breaks in a tensed
ecstasy that moves and satisfies.

Shadow makes a fulcrum of its own body
and stretches into more places
than the coinage of the day.

The notes that lay most naturally,
being composed through, for them
the dream may not have been dreamt out,

soundscape of dotted rhythms and heavy
blows, with drums holding the home key,
and a horn that has heard what the violin wanted.

The Shadow Lord

Sand-webs buff and blue, white hedges,
a green so young it is yellow;

keepsake of a two-foot flag,
or a gold-banded Caroline hat,
round, with lace edges.

It is a map would singe your eyebrows
and make a gallows of your person
with all the neatness and plenty
of a charity coffin.

Its Irish filters and airy titles
and vertical attachments
like old-throated limes, the very trees
which calmly looked on at the tumult.

Among the endless paper
you are a break-handled pike
who steady your right hand
on your left hip, incite

my whole sounding body
to move in flavoured step,
lifted and put down by

your arm's vernacular necklace
not yet bared of muscle,
farm without bounds or a bush

on the same, semi-naked counties
that the soonest fires were on.

The Blood Changer

I prayed your clenched yolk out of purgatory:

this high-up, pearl-hard paschal-time,
I stand in the old sun-made sun-substance,
you in the new, yet hewn together
like sleek archangel wings.

When you killed, nests of pale bloom
shone in your steep face, winter-stunned,
by falling out of the infinite into yourself:

just day partaking of the far-up sky
talking to the uptilted world in me.

Warm and dead, impregnating like rain,
your spark of white release loomed
in the heavier red of the side-passage, one
with the nails, moulding the wound
and utmost waters of my unopened life.

Praying Male Figurine

The bookend of the year
was shining you away. At your street junction
which does not form a perfect cross
to deny the bitter wind,

I raised your half-collar
like a triplet of windows
for an ampler intake of light,
I, a false keyhole,

whose key turns fourteen tongues at once,
preferring to die upon each other's swords,
was held on your wooden pillow
by snow-ducts singing from scrolls.

More than a Letter

Sleep-knotted as if folded in prayer,
your feet close together in the ballet-length
clouds, a young girl's sky of dead kisses
fastens your groomless night.

Your room has no exit, from the outside
only one label, on an iron gate where
poppies rot. I had almost forgotten
your glance, once and for all.

The blood-move of your hand was not free
but freed. We sat under an oak-tree behind
English lines, where you arrive
by old-fashioned side-roads, and the leaves
are beginning to look as if they want to fall.

Like a sub-citizen perpetually with me,
your sleek body suits you with its soldier-silk
everywhere, destroyed horizons that re-form themselves
further on. Even saying words you believe to be
the last, kisses badly the underbed of my mind.

The Sickness of the Cloth

Summer is your worst hour.
When everything has turned completely golden
you will recover your blue, transparent sky:
when the gardens of evening
begin to suffer, your olive-clothed hillsides
will taste of honey and dawn.

Now it rains even though God
doesn't want it to. A phantom river
feeds the cowed, impoverished city;
we see in looking-from squares
the souls of all who used to cross them.

Crosses look like missiles,
the rose-coloured blotches
of feeble Republican bombings
embroider a Liberal flag.

Where the unsurfaced road loops sharply
a sea of fruit and dark flesh
made for the moon is born. Its silence
deadens two contrary musics,
but its tongue is luminous.

From November to November
the nights of reeds in shadow
exchange sunflowers, the moons of that place
are beautiful as Joseph,
and thousands of winged insects
spread myrtle there, each living cell
thawed by the last, still-bearing warmth.

The Jasmine-Picker

Time stopped watching
wherever it comes from
and nowhere touched.

All winter movements
swooped out of their slumber:
the facile hand that braided
the barbed wire forgot
the murmur of roses.

The string of doves
around her neck
swam and breast-fed
at every level of his heart.

His face stayed ineloquent,
rolled up, sowing
a year's worth
of time-bound children.

Their insurgent faces
guarded by slaves
to give the impression
of mastery over a country.

The prayerless non-colour
of the provincial hearses
established their beloved dust
around the ring of death
like colour squeezed
from a mauve
and willow-green flower.

So, disinvited,
the wrist-pleats' downward swing
soared above the enchantment
of a world trying to live.

Columbarium

A sudden crop of smiles,
miniature full moons,
fell into the nearly full
shadow on all those faces.

Light in the right places
hardened as it met the air
or pressed a brown fire close
to the chandeliers in their Holland bags.

An afterness that they had kissed
flowed in the shapely leaves.
My breast was ready to run or lie
or strip my hat swinging by its ribbons.

Passing jewels ripened
on the outskirts of my untried mouth:
my back printed thick
freed the road till it disappeared.

Part Five

SHANNON'S RECOVERY

Shannon's Recovery

Moon-plunge
into the still river-like
womb-opening.

Father with your smooth lip
my graveless departure,
swallow its stillness.

Curve south, dearly matched
road that crossed
miles of my heart.

Be the three-way loved one
gone, a branch remembered
for its tugging shade,

its pencil-faint patches
drawing small frames
in a silver direction.

Touch me on every side,
sides of the living mountain,
my middle name in width.

And welcome back
ourselves, our own almost,
the coldness of my mouth now.

The Latissimus Station

Days which were bitterly summer
were miracles as such.
I could not bear to remove
the keys of the blood, the hands
that sealed me in, the truth
that held me close, that antiquated kiss.

I locked myself into your open
side, your pierced wine-cask,
the hollowed-out steps in your body
whose last step is the peace
of your mouth.

Both stones and a wall, we were offered
as dead in the garden, so let's
be dead: because I did not first
pour out water, you now
withhold your blood, releasing
each contraction like a bomb.

What the Month Brings

Daybreak streets, so stone,
birth is nothing but you.
My head feels grown to your pillow.
I have taken your sound into my bloodstream
as far as nights can go,
their unnatural colours running in the rain,
airless, windless, noiseless and unstained
as the beat of the morning's heart.

Your blossoms are the only light
and cannot leave me,
though, like a paused swallow,
I breathe and stop breathing,
closing my skin to December roads
unseen since late September.

Hands that cooled
like an easy-to-come-by sea
in the first phase of winter,
both old and not old, touch
their kissed and re-kissed
thigh-smoothed fingers
to the forehead's crossed-out root:

while softened earth,
earth-red from its air burial,
pulls down spring like a memory.

The Tamarind Tree

2 January 1996

The lowest string of winter beggars my muse:
his mind is the moon that I am selling land on.
My crooked soul breathes its life air from his heels
when it should worship the desireless horizon.

Like a bird sitting with another bird
within the same bodily tree, like the swan
who knows the art of sucking milk
out of a mixture of milk and water, the sun

decreasing fails to rob me, my steel-framed heart
leaves unprayed for the planets of his ankles,
the polished animals of his eyelids.

But soon, on the Sunday called Laetare, impure ghosts
wearing the skins of us almsgiving trees
will pass like heraldic nettles into the unmixed sunray.

Creggan Churchyard

On his bared knee, this written kiss,
wind without rain, that throws its voice
along a furrow, crystal-clear
into the harp-like breast of graves in grass.

On the high stoneless lip of the glen,
white poppies, diamond bullets, varnish the joints of time,
where my lord-lady, milordess, ringed my hand feudally,
dried my secret hand with his stone eye.

The Society of the Bomb

The sleep of her lover is her sleep:
it warms her and brings her out to people
like half-making love or the wider now,
exceptionally sunlit spring.

Before violence was actually offered
to us, we followed a trail of words
into the daylight, those palest and clearest
blues, and all the snow to come.

The Temple of Janus

Now, in this bloodless city, this Possession Island,
the wounds of the monk-soldiers seem like ornaments,
or late, cosmetic concessions;
and bodies slide the length of their shrouds
into outstretched arms.
And we are forced to grip the shrouds
with our teeth, we try to keep them warm
with a panel of our sleeves, the hands which hang
powerful and helpless, at the end of arms.
The heads from which all pain
has disappeared, the eyes almost white,
in these last skirmishes, these alternations
of Golgothas and fairs.

Wan-looking Christs shown full-face
with crow-black beards and thin little
sunburnt angels,
so generously naked, very nude Mercuries,
athletic young men at the mercy of their skin,
with their interlaced limbs
they create an arch,
the essence of a nation
in a bath of sand.

You talk to me of the country's hostilities
as though describing a harvest,
or a wedding during Advent
to a woman holding a broken lute:
because it was him,
because it was me, the crowd formed a hedge
which took his reds and blues as accidents.

In the secrecy of the house
he would let the medianoche fabric fall,
or appear crushed, the opposite of an Italian,
serenely revealing his side.

Lake in Middle Shadow

Here it is fully nighttime, and you are twice dead,
the air in which your surfaces are clothed
is thinner by half, wholly cloudy air
to which you have turned your back. As a leaf
reversed leaves a trace of itself
under its branch, so you are the side
of the world to which I am turned —
twin vein of my bud, diameter of my sky.

Does this sky appear to you whiter than that
above you, translucent like linen, the colour
of the horizon, continuing to take in
images located beyond it? Some measure
of conscious violence re-ignites
the percussed air, showing me your face,
part by part, the air of your face,
the parts that are turned towards these streets.

As when we look from squares into doorways,
bearing the radiance of the air, each makes
an angle for something not touched
by the principal light. Each sends out
a derivative shadow imprinted like a cross,
generated by the air, the target and the magnet,
your O's and A's, open at the top,
travelling like manna the double sky.

Brighter when viewed along the path of the wind,
they seem to tinge its path with the semblance
of their colour, till each root is surrounded
by a rainbow of equal height. And where the ray
is intersected and destroyed, the final shadows
share in the original colour, even taking on
more blue, as if wishing to be avenged,
on the water that runs most narrowly,

which is most receptive to the first or any shadow,
in shadowy rain lets its bed be seen,
in luminous, regains its ancient bed. An interval
of dense air fights with the span of your shoulders,
runs them together into my eye like the neck
of a captive animal. But you, in a single glance,
will be able to picture yourself again as a lover,
your longest fingers, letting your arms fall.

Film-Still

The gesture of to-be-looked-at-ness
has gone on, though the space inside it
is where his body stood.

When the eyes of every face we have kissed
have been covered with leaves, his eyes
open in his cupped hands, his chest
buds like a flower, in the new depthlessness
of a more reproduced world, frozen encounter
with what we may become.

I tell by looking at him that time has passed,
he takes time and turns it into a place,
both resolute and exhausted, so unnervingly human,
to be used like colour, catching two colours
in the same movement, image and image-maker.

It was my hand made these marks but not
my handwriting; it was the striped light
valorising the internal, female shadows,
till the signpost makes a bond with the real shadow,
and every fold, drape, shadow and even leaf,
is anchored in the vineyard of consciousness.

My mind, no longer able to be unified,
pulls into it, a gun held and another pointed;
cold relic of earth and harvest, unfashionable
felt-room unfixed and refixed, not newsworthy before,
but the cured forest burned out over it.

Stone Orchard

The source of the fragrance is not the promise
of the reddish bed, edged by blackness:
your forest-covered shoulders double daylight.
Touch by touch you protect the hours, a week
of days that flow together by their own weight.

Corner room, north porch floored with brick,
your clean world of memory has no surface
but breaking, its sea-waves and sea-made
sand-dunes drive out of it the creature water —
that cloud-beginner that asks nature
for something she cannot give . . .

Youth-opening flowers fade
on the seed to come; your heart
is the slight branch by which alone
the tree gains height.

Like two cities formed by two loves,
your marble residue suspended
in a medium of death, takes revenge
for that revenge, in the workmanship
of its accidentally uninvaded streets.

Month of snow once visibly receding
from the field of existence; feast of remembrance
spun round by guards; let your mythical
exhaustion never finish, let your barns
come down and your views come out.

The Birthday of Monday

I have kissed the door behind which he is sleeping.
I am within two streets of where he lies,
the skin on his back blackened and cured
by all weathers.

He moves only his tongue,
saying goodbye many times,
his tongue has a little salt about it.

A net of leather rests on his head
holding his muzzle closed, so his head
seems wrapped in veils or self-wrapped
veils itself as a fermenting moment
between cloud and edgeless cloud.

He leans upon a brush of free flame,
without colour, making a cool mould
that will be there when he is gone.

He bruises his sides against walls too close together,
a breadth of land into which he is caught
and fitted like an unfamiliar voice.

His eyes are frozen open, young enough eyes,
shallow bowls of lasting snow, frosted paths,
pencils of ice.

His lips, a line of cinder-dry iron,
dustless, too much touched, become
a red pool of comfort, one window wide.

A rush of earthbound, makeshift air
that cannot be bitten by his mouth
soothes his lungs.

The shadows of his hair
are avenues of powdered shell,
every wind-inspired movement of branch
brings an axe-blemish to them.

He has left me a fresh-robbed word,
a small flat gift; an old word
unsoftened by sun. His tongue cannot
make the word written into his body smoother.

Like a hand swept over candles,
giving pain neatly,
it feeds me dust and then sucks its fill;
it is born into my winter kimono
like a lightless harbour that lets it land,
that pays out the distance and takes cover
behind it.

But its name has not explained
how ready-to-rain felt to the full grown day;
how stars burned, a galaxy of scars,

shedding pin-scratch yellow,
how I stroked the place between his eyes,
shading the muscle against the bone,
the weight of his fingers and their hope in mine.

We had fed on flowers, summer's fake
irises, chrysanthemums trained to entrap
the breeze — not peace, but armistice,
whose tarnished white vestment
escapes its baptism:

like a tapered river, running only
on its heart, that has swallowed itself
in the buried fields
of almost the last waves;

like a leaf waiting
for another war to pass.

Mantilla

for Shane Murphy

My resurrective verses shed people
and reinforced each summer.
I saw their time as my own time,
I said, this day will penetrate
those other days, using a thorn
to remove a thorn in the harness
of my mind where anyone's touch
stemmed my dreams.
                    From below
to above all decay I stated
my contentless name and held
the taste as though it were dying
all over true in the one day light.

My sound world was a vassal state,
a tightly bonded lattice of water
sealed with cunning to rear
the bridge of breathing.
                   And my raw
mouth a non-key of spring, a cousin
sometimes source, my signature
vibrational as parish flowers.

Sky Portrait

for Jane

Perhaps this is his night, his deathlessness,
seeing eleven moons at once passing
life after life.
Not across a small sky
in a small universe, but the medium blue
sense of hearing whose skin
is the moving air.

Perhaps the whole movement of our earth
around its sun takes place inside him,
and the total sunshine
of millions of suns
saves him from living even momentarily:

as a river is worshipped by its water;
as a bird always prays for its cloud;
as a love-laden wind that is shown
a deserving planet will never be re-born.